I HAVE CROSSED AN OCEAN

Grace Nichols was born in Guyana, and has lived in Britain since 1977. Her first collection, *I is a Long Memoried Woman* (1983) won the Commonwealth Poetry Prize. This was followed by four collections with Virago, *The Fat Black Woman's Poems* (1984), *Lazy Thoughts of a Lazy Woman* (1989), *Sunris* (1996), winner of the Guyana Prize, and *Startling the Flying Fish* (2006), poems which tell the story of the Caribbean, along with several poetry books for younger readers, including *Come on into My Tropical Garden* (1988), *Give Yourself a Hug* (1994), *Everybody Got a Gift* (2005) and *Cosmic Disco* (2013). Her four most recent poetry books are published by Bloodaxe: *Picasso, I Want My Face Back* (2009), *I Have Crossed an Ocean: Selected Poems* (2010), *The Insomnia Poems* (2017), and *Passport from Here to There* (2020), a Poetry Book Society Special Commendation. She was poet-in-residence at the Tate Gallery, London in 1999-2000, and received a Cholmondeley Award for her work in 2001. She lives in Sussex with the poet John Agard and their family.

GRACE NICHOLS

I Have Crossed an Ocean

SELECTED POEMS

BLOODAXE BOOKS

ISBN: 978 1 85224 858 1

First published 2010 by
Bloodaxe Books Ltd,
Eastburn,
South Park,
Hexham,
Northumberland NE46 1BS.

Reprinted 2013, 2016, 2017, 2020

www.bloodaxebooks.com
For further information about Bloodaxe titles
please visit our website or write to
the above address for a catalogue.

Supported by
ARTS COUNCIL
ENGLAND

Cover design: Neil Astley & Pamela Robertson-Pearce.

This is a digital reprint of the 2010 Bloodaxe edition.

For John, Lesley, Kalera and Yansan,
and for my sisters and brother,
Avril, Valerie, Dennis and Claire

ACKNOWLEDGEMENTS

This book includes poems which Grace Nichols has herself chosen from her previous collections: *I Is a Long-Memoried Woman* (Karnak House, 1983); *The Fat Black Woman's Poems* (1984), *Lazy Thoughts of a Lazy Woman* (1989), *Sunris* (1996) and *Startling the Flying Fish* (2006) – all published by Virago. The poems for younger readers are from the following books: *Come On Into My Tropical Garden* (A&C Black, 1988), *No Hickory No Dickory No Dock* (Puffin/Viking 1991), *Give Yourself a Hug* (A&C Black, 1994), *The Poet Cat* (Bloomsbury, 2000), *Paint Me a Poem* (A&C Black, 2004) and *Everybody Got a Gift* (new and selected, A&C Black, 2004).

Later collections by Grace Nichols, *Picasso, I Want My Face Back* (2009) and *The Insomnia Poems* (2017), are published by Bloodaxe Books separately from this book.

CONTENTS

from

I IS A LONG-MEMORIED WOMAN

WOMAN

(1983)

Even in dreams I will submerge myself
swimming like one possessed
back and forth across that course
strewing it with sweet smelling flowers –
one for everyone who made the journey

One Continent to Another

(extract)

Like the yesterday of creation morning
she had imagined this new world to be
bereft of fecundity

No she wasn't prepared
for the sea that lashed
fire that seared
solid earth that delivered
her up
birds that flew
not wanting to see the utter
rawness of life everywhere

and the men who seed the children
she wasn't prepared for that look
in their eye –
that loss of deep man pride

Now she stoops
in green canefields
piecing the life she would lead

Days That Fell

And yet
And yet

the cutlass in her hand
could not cut through
the days that fell
like bramble

and the destruction that
threatened to choke
within
as she leaned closer to
the earth
seeking some truth
unarmed against the noon

*

We must hold fast to dreams
We must be patient
from the crouching of those huts
from the sprouting of these fields
We can emerge

all revolutions are rooted in dreams

Waterpot

The daily going out
and coming in
always being hurried
along
like like... cattle

In the evenings
returning from the fields
she tried hard to walk
like a woman
pulling herself erect
with every three or four
steps
pulling herself together
holding herself like
royal cane

And the overseer
hurrying them along
in the quickening darkness

And the overseer sneering
them along in the quickening
darkness

sneered at the pathetic –
the pathetic display
of dignity

O but look
there's a waterpot growing
from her head

Each Time They Came

Ibo/Yoruba
Ashanti/Fanti
Mane

Each time they came
she went out to see them –
the new arrivals
faces full of old incisions
calves grooved from shackles
ankles swollen
from the pain

Each time they came
she made as if
to touch them
the new arrivals
her own lips
moving
in a dreaming
kind of prayer

*

How can I eulogise their names?
what dance of mourning
can I make?

Taint

But I was stolen by men
the colour of my own skin
borne away by men
whose heels had become hoofs
whose hands had turned talcons

Bearing me down
    to the trail
        of darkness

But I was traded by men
the colour of my own skin
traded like a fowl   like a goat
like a sack of kernels I was traded
for beads   for pans   for trinkets?

No it isn't easy to forget
what we refuse to remember –
daily I rinse the taint
of treachery from my mouth

Sacred Flame

Our women
the ones I left behind
always know the taste
of their own strength —
bitter at times it might be

But I
armed only with
my mother's smile
must be forever gathering
my life together like scattered beads

*

What was your secret mother —
the one that made you a woman
and not just Obafemi's wife

With your thighs you gave
a generation of beautiful children

With your mind you willed the crops
commanding a good harvest

With your hands and heart
plantain soup and love

But the sacred flame of your woman's
kra you gave to no man, mother

Perhaps that was the secret then —
the one that made you a woman
and not just Obafemi's wife

Without Song

The faces of the children
    are small and stricken and black
They have fallen
into exile
moving without song
or prayer

They have fallen
into mourning
moving to the shrouds
of tares

The faces of the children
    are small and stricken and black

They have fallen
into silence
uttering no cry
laying no blame

And the sun burns to copper
yet the rains, the rains gather
like diamonds
in the fleece of their hair

Ala

Face up
they hold her naked body
to the ground
arms and legs spread-eagle
each tie with rope to stake

Then they coat her
in sweet molasses
and call us out to see –
the rebel-woman who
with a pin, stick the soft mould
of her own child's head

Sending the newborn soul
winging its way
back to Africa – free –
they call us out
to see the fate of all us –
rebel women

the slow and painful
picking away of the flesh
by red and pitiless ants

but while the sun blind her
with his fury
we the women sing
and weep as we work

'O Ala,
Uzo is due to join you
to return to the pocket of your womb

O Ala
Mother who gives
and receives again in death

Gracious one
have sympathy
let her enter
let her rest'

Sugar Cane

1

There is something
about sugarcane

He isn't what
he seem –

indifferent hard
and sheathed in blades

his waving arms
is a sign for help

his skin thick
only to protect
the juice inside
himself

2

His colour
is the aura
of jaundice
when he ripe

he shiver
like ague
when it rain

he suffer
from bellywork
burning fever
and delirium

just before
the hurricane
strike
smashing him to pieces

3

Growing up
is an art

he don't have
any control of

it is us
who groom and
weed him

who stick him
in the earth
in the first place

and when he
growing tall

with the help
of the sun
and rain

we feel the
need to strangle
the life

out of him

But either way he can't survive

4

Slowly
painfully
sugar
cane
pushes
his
knotted
joints
upwards
from
the
earth
slowly
painfully
he
comes
to learn
the
truth
about
himself
the
crimes
committed
in
his
name

5

He cast his shadow
to the earth

the wind is
his only mistress

I hear them
moving
in rustling tones

she shakes
his hard reserve

smoothing
stroking
caressing
all his length
shamelessly

I crouch
below them
quietly

Like a Flame

Raising up
from my weeding
of ripening cane

my eyes
make four
with this man

there ain't
no reason
to laugh

but
I laughing
in confusion

his hands
soft his words
quick his lips
curling as in
prayer

I nod

I like this man

Tonight
I go to meet him
life a flame

Up My Spine

I see the old dry-head woman
leaning on her hoe
twist-up and shaky like a cripple-insect

I see her ravaged skin
the stripes of mould where the whip fall –
hard

I see her missing toe
her jut-out hipbone
from way back time when she had a fall

I see the old dry-head woman
leaning on her hoe
twist-up and shaky like a cripple-insect –

I see the pit of her eye
I hear her rattle bone laugh
putting a chill up my spine

I Coming Back

I coming back 'Massa'
I coming back

mistress of the underworld
I coming back

colour and shape
of all that is evil
I coming back

dog howling outside
yuh window
I coming back

ball-a-fire
and skinless higue
I coming back

hiss in yuh ear
and prick in yuh skin
I coming back

bone in yuh throat
and laugh in yuh skull
I coming back

I coming back 'Massa'
I coming back

Night Is Her Robe

Night is her robe
Moon is her element

Quivering and alert
she's stepping out behind
the fields of sugarcane

She's stepping out softly
she's stepping out carefully
she's bending / she's stalking
she's flitting / she's crawling

Quivering and alert
she's coming to the edge
of her island forest

Now with all the care
of a herbalist
she's gathering strange weeds
wild root
leaves with the property
both to harm and to heal

Quivering and alert
Quivering and alert
she's leaving the edge
of her island forest

Skin-Teeth

Not every skin-teeth
is a smile 'Massa'

if you see me smiling
when you pass

if you see me bending
when you ask

Know that I smile
know that I bend
only the better
to rise and strike
again

Love Act

She enter into his Great House
her see-far looking eyes
unassuming

He fix her with his glassy stare
and feel the thin fire in his blood
awakening

Soon she is the fuel
that keep them all going

He/his mistresswife/and his
children who take to her breasts
like leeches

He want to tower above her
want her to raise her ebony
haunches and when she does
he think she can be trusted
and drinks her in

And his mistresswife
spending her days in rings
of vacant smiling
is glad to be rid of the
loveact

But time pass/es

Her sorcery cut them
like a whip

She hide her triumph
and slowly stir the hate
of poison in

In My Name

Heavy with child

belly
an arc
of black moon

I squat over
dry plantain leaves

and command the earth
to receive you

in my name
in my blood

to receive you
my curled bean

my tainted

perfect child

                    my bastard fruit
                    my seedling
                    my sea grape
                    my strange mulatto
                    my little bloodling

Let the snake slipping in deep grass
be dumb before you

Let the centipede writhe and shrivel
in its tracks

Let the evil one strangle on his own tongue
even as he sets his eyes upon you

For with my blood
I've cleansed you
and with my tears
I've pooled the river Niger

now my sweet one it is for you to swim

Yemanji

It was here by the riverside
I came upon Yemanji
Mother of all beings sprawled
upon the rivershore, her long
breasts (insulted by her husband)
oozing milk that lapped and flowed

Yemanji
Mother of seas
Goddess of rivers
I will pay homage to you
you who bless your followers
with an abundance of children
you whose temple rests like a lotus
in Ibidan, you whose waters flow down
the River Ogun, past the cities of Abeokuta
and Oyo

Yemanji
Mother of Shango
Mother of the long breasts
of milk and sorrow

Sacred be your river stones.

Like Anansi

I was the Ashanti spider

woman-keeper
of dreams
tenacious
opalescent
dark eyes
unblinking

waiting
with a long
and naked fury

then you came
like Anansi
you came

calm and cunning
as a madman

not at all
what I was expecting

bells hung
from your little waist
an ornate flute

beads and feathers
stood in your cap
and I laughed at you

Of Golden Gods

Alone
skull as empty as a gobi
I watch my chameleon spirit
take its exit
shapely as a distant breeze
across the face of heaven

deepening
from azure
to indigo darkness
circling slowly the
archipelago
of burnished green

moving from land to sea
from swamp to Southern
vastness
where the rains have been
falling hardest
in the pit of the serpent jungle

up, past the Inca ruins
and back again
drifting onto Mexican plains

the crumbling of golden gods
and Aztec rites
speak for themselves
that, and before, the
genocides –
all a prelude to my time.

I Will Enter

Singed by a flight of scarlet ibises
blinded like a grasshopper by the rains

tattered and hungry
you took me in

gave me cassava bread
and cassiri

a hammock to sleep in

a blanket woven by
your own hands
rich with embroidery

          *

I will enter
I will enter

through the Indian forest
of your hair

through the passage of your
wary watchful eyes

through the bitterness
of your cassava touch
I will enter

And when you are moonsick
I will bleed with you

But wait
like a broken flute
your tongue is silent
your eyes speak of an
ancient weariness
I too have known
memory is written
in each crumpled fold
you can still remember
how they pitted gun against
arrow
steel against stillness

Stunned by their demands
for gold

And so you'll talk no more
of Amalivaca
or the mystery of his strange
rock writings

No more of Kaie
brave old chief who took
to sacrifice on behalf
of his tribe
rushing the falls before
the great Makonima's eye

This Kingdom

This Kingdom Will Not Reign
Forever

Cool winds blow
softly

in brilliant sunshine
fruits pulse
flowers flame

mountains shade to
purple

the great House
with its palm and orange
groves
sturdy

and the sea encircling
all
is a spectrum of blue
jewels
shimmering and skirting

But Beware

Soft winds can turn
volatile
can merge with rains
can turn hurricane

Mountains can erupt
sulphur springs
bubbling quick
and hot

like bile spilling
from a witch's cauldron

Swamps can send plagues
dysentry, fevers

plantations can perish

lands turn barren

And the white man
no longer at ease
with the faint drum/
beat

no longer indifferent
to the sweating sun/
heat

can leave exhausted
or
turn his thoughts
to death

And we
the rage growing
like the chiggers
in our feet

can wait
or
take our freedom

whatever happens

This Kingdom Will Not Reign
Forever

Wind a Change

Wind a change
blow soft but
steadfast

ripple the spears
of sugar cane
stir slow the leaves
of indigo

Dance
waltz
soothe
this old mud-wattle
hut
bring if you can
the smell of Dahomey
again

Wind a change
cool mountain water
open river flower

But pass easy
up the big house
way
let them sleep
they happy white sleep

Yes, Wind a change
keep yuh coming fire
secret

Omen

I require an omen, a signal
I kyan not work this craft
on my own strength

alligator teeth
and feathers
old root and powder

I kyan not work this craft
this magic black
on my own strength

Dahomey lurking in my shadows
Yoruba lurking in my shadows
Ashanti lurking in my shadows

I am confused
I lust for guidance
a signal, a small omen
perhaps a bird picking
at my roof

                    *

All is silent now
silent the fields
silent the canes
silent the drum
silent the blades
silent the sea
turning back to silence
a fatalistic rising siletnce

What's that sound? What's that flame?

Holding My Beads

Unforgiving as the course of justice
Inerasable as my scars and fate
I am here
a woman... with all my lives
strung out like beads
                              before me
It isn't privilege or pity
that I seek
It isn't reverence or safety
quick happiness or purity
                              but
the power to be what I am/a woman
charting my own futures/ a woman
holding my beads in my hand

Epilogue

I have crossed an ocean
I have lost my tongue
From the root of the old one
A new one has sprung

from

THE FAT BLACK
WOMAN'S POEMS

(1984)

Price We Pay for the Sun

These islands
not picture postcards
for unravelling tourist
you know
these islands real
more real
than flesh and blood
past stone
past foam
these islands split
bone

my mother's breasts
like sleeping volcanoes
who know
what kinda sulph-furious
cancer tricking her
below
while the wind
constantly whipping
my father's tears
to salty hurricanes
and my grandmothers croon
sifting sand
water mirroring palm

Poverty is the price
we pay for the sun girl
run come

Those Women

Cut and contriving women
hauling fresh shrimps
up in their seines

standing waist deep
in the brown voluptuous
water of their own element

how I remember those women
sweeping in the childish rivers
of my eyes

and the fish slipping
like eels
through their laughing thighs

The candlefly

The candlefly
always came at night
blinking the ceiling
with its small searchlight

as a child I stared up
uneasily through the darkness
remembering the old folk saying

Candlefly means
a stranger will come
a stranger will visit

still I couldn't be comforted
the candlefly was both a magic
and a menace

a creature with a mission

a flickering stranger

                    not unlike death

Iguana Memory

Saw an iguana once
when I was very small
in our backdam backyard
came rustling across my path

green like moving newleaf sunlight

big like big big lizard
with more legs than centipede
so it seemed to me
and it must have stopped a while
eyes meeting mine
iguana and child locked in a brief
split moment happening
before it went hurrying

        for the green of its life

Star-apple

Deepest purple
or pale green white
the star-apple is a sweet fruit
with a sweet star brimming centre
and a turn back skin
that always left me sweetly
sticky mouth

Be a Butterfly

Don't be a kyatta-pilla
Be a butterfly
old preacher screamed
to illustrate his sermon
of Jesus and the higher life

rivulets of well-earned
sweat sliding down
his muscly mahogany face
in the half-empty school church
we sat shaking with muffling
laughter
watching our mother trying to save
herself from joining the wave

only our father remaining poker face
and afterwards we always went home to
split peas Sunday soup
with dumplings, fufu and pigtail

Don't be a kyatta-pilla
Be a butterfly
Be a butterfly

That was de life preacher
and you was right

Back Home Contemplation

There is more to heaven
than meet the eye
there is more to sea
than watch the sky
there is more to earth
than dream the mind

O my eye

The heavens are blue
but the sun is murderous
the sea is calm
but the waves reap havoc
the earth is firm
but trees dance shadows
and bush eyes turn

Praise Song for My Mother

You were
water to me
deep and bold and fathoming

You were
moon's eye to me
pull and grained and mantling

You were
sunrise to me
rise and warm and streaming

You were
the fish's red gill to me
the flame tree's spread to me
the crab's leg/the fried plantain smell
                         replenishing replenishing

Go to your wide futures, you said

Like a Beacon

In London
every now and then
I get this craving
for my mother's food
I leave art galleries
in search of plantains
saltfish/sweet potatoes

I need this link

I need this touch
of home
swinging my bag
like a beacon
against the cold

Island Man

(for a Caribbean island man in London
who still wakes up to the sound of the sea)

Morning
and island man wakes up
to the sound of blue surf
in his head
the steady breaking and wombing

wild seabirds
and fishermen pushing out to sea
the sun surfacing defiantly

from the east
of his small emerald island
he always comes back   groggily groggily

Comes back to sands
of a grey metallic soar
                              to surge of wheels
to dull North Circular roar

muffling muffling
his crumpled pillow waves
island man heaves himself

Another London day

Spring

After two unpredictable spells
of influenza that winter
I was taking no chances
(not even to put the rubbish outside)

pulling on my old black jacket
resolutely winding
a scarf round and round my neck
winter rituals I had grown to
accept
with all the courage of an unemerged
butterfly
I unbolted the door and stepped outside

only to have that daffodil baby
kick me in the eye

Waiting for Thelma's laughter

(for Thelma, my West Indian born Afro-American neighbour)

You wanna take the world in hand
and fix it up
the way you fix your living room

You wanna reach out and crush
life's big and small injustices
in the fire and honey of your hands

You wanna scream
cause your head's too small
for your dreams

And the children running around
             acting like lil clowns
                  breaking the furniture down

While I sit through it all
watching you
knowing anytime now

Your laughter's gonna come
to drown and heal us all

Winter Thoughts

I've reduced the sun
to the neat oblong of fire
in my living room

I've reduced the little
flesh tongues of the vagina
to the pimpled grate
and the reddening licking
flames

I've reduced the sea
to the throbbing fruit
in me

And outside
the old rose tree
is once again winterdying

While I lay here sprawled
thinking
how sex and death
are always at the heart
of living

Two Old Black Men on a Leicester Square Park Bench

What do you dream of you
old black men sitting
on park benches staunchly
wrapped up in scarves
and coats of silence
eyes far away from the cold
grey and strutting
pigeon
ashy fingers trembling
(though it's said that the old
hardly ever feel the cold)

do you dream revolutions
you could have forged
or mourn some sunfull woman
you might have known
a hibiscus flower
ghost memories of desire

O it's easy
to rainbow the past
after all the letters from
home spoke of hardships

and the sun was traded long ago

The Fat Black Woman's Cycle

The Assertion

Heavy as a whale
eyes beady with contempt
and a kind of fire of love
the fat black woman sits
on the golden stool
and refuses to move

the white robed chiefs
are resigned
in their postures of resignation

the fat black woman's fingers
are creased in gold
body ringed in folds
pulse beat at her throat

This is my birthright
says the fat black woman
giving a fat black chuckle
showing her fat black toes

The Fat Black Woman's Motto
on Her Bedroom Door

IT'S BETTER TO DIE IN THE FLESH OF HOPE
THAN TO LIVE IN THE SLIMNESS OF DESPAIR

The Fat Black Woman Goes Shopping

Shopping in London winter
is a real drag for the fat black woman
going from store to store
in search of accommodating clothes
and de weather so cold

Look at the frozen thin mannequins
fixing her with grin
and de pretty face salesgals
exchanging slimming glances
thinking she don't notice

Lord is aggravating

Nothing soft and bright and billowing
to flow like breezy sunlight
when she walking

The fat black woman curses in Swahili/Yoruba
and nation language under her breathing
all this journeying and journeying

The fat black woman could only conclude
that when it come to fashion
the choice is lean

                Nothing much beyond size 14

A Fat Poem

Fat is
as fat is
as fat is

Fat does
as fat thinks

Fat feels
as fat please

Fat believes

        Fat is to butter
        as milk is to cream
        fat is to sugar
        as pud is to steam

Fat is a dream
in times of lean

        fat is a darling
        a dumpling
        a squeeze
        fat is cuddles
        up a baby's sleeve

        and fat speaks for itself

Tropical Death

The fat black woman want
a brilliant tropical death
not a cold sojourn
in some North Europe far/forlorn

The fat black woman want
some heat/hibiscus at her feet
blue sea dress
to wrap her neat

The fat black woman want
some bawl
no quiet jerk tear wiping
a polite hearse withdrawal

The fat black woman want
all her dead rights
first night
third night
nine night
all the sleepless droning
red-eyed wake nights

In the heart
of her mother's sweetbreast
In the shade
of the sun leaf's cool bless
In the bloom
of her people's bloodrest

the fat black woman want
a brilliant tropical death yes

Invitation

1

If my fat
was too much for me
I would have told you
I would have lost a stone
or two

I would have gone jogging
even when it was fogging
I would have weighed in
sitting the bathroom scale
with my tail tucked in

I would have dieted
more care than a diabetic

But as it is
I'm feeling fine
feel no need
to change my lines
when I move I'm target light

Come up and see me sometime

2

Come up and see me sometime
Come up and see me sometime

My breasts are huge exciting
amnions of watermelon
                 your hands can't cup
my thighs are twin seals
                 fat slick pups
there's a purple cherry
below the blues
                 of my black seabelly
there's a mole that gets a ride
each time I shift the heritage
of my behind

Come up and see me sometime

Thoughts Drifting Through the Fat Black Woman's Head While Having a Full Bubble Bath

Steatopygous sky
Steatopygous sea
Steatopygous waves
Steatopygous me

O how I long to place my foot
on the head of anthropology

to swig my breasts
in the face of history

to scrub my back
with the dogma of theology

to put my soap
in the slimming industry's
profitsome spoke

Steatopygous sky
Steatopygous sea
Steatopygous waves
Steatopygous me

The Fat Black Woman's Instructions to a Suitor

Do the boogie-woogie
Do the hop
Do the Charlestown
Do the rock
Do the chicken funky
Do the foxtrot

Do the tango
Drop yourself like a mango
Do the minuet
Spin me a good ole pirouette
Do the highland fling
Get down baby
Do that limbo thing

After doing all that and maybe mo
hope you have a little energy left
to carry me across the threshold

Small Questions Asked by the Fat Black Woman

Will the rains
cleanse the earth of shrapnel
and wasted shells

will the seas
toss up bright fish
in wave on wave of toxic shoal

will the waters
seep the shore

feeding slowly the greying
angry roots

will trees bear fruit

will I like Eve
be tempted once again
if I survive

from

LAZY THOUGHTS OF
A LAZY WOMAN

(1989)

Dust

Dust has a right to settle
Milk the right to curdle
Cheese the right to turn green
Scum and fungi are rich words.

Grease

Grease steals in like a lover
over the body of my oven.
Grease kisses the knobs
of my stove.
Grease plays with the small
hands of my spoons.
Grease caresses the skin
of my table-cloth,
laying claim to my every crease.
Grease reassures me that life
is naturally sticky.

Grease is obviously having an affair with me.

With Apologies to Hamlet

To pee or not to pee
That is the question

Whether it's sensibler in the mind
To suffer for sake of verse
The discomforting slings
Of a full and pressing bladder
Or to break poetic thought for loo
As a course of matter
And by apee-sing end it

In Spite of Me

In spite of me
the women in me
slip free
of the charmed circle
of my moulding

Look at Graceful eh!
long skirts, legs crossed
all smiles
articulating ethnic attentiveness
'Graceful is as graceful is,'
I mock, but Graceful
just goes on being graceful

And Indiscreet
who can stop Indiscreet
from acting indiscreet
wearing her womb on her sleeve
telling the details of her sullied
secrets. Her moves, her searches
her tiresome cosmic wetness.

Obsessional at least
has the good sense
to stay put at home
head tied, cloth soaked in lemon juice,
to keep her thoughts at bay
Obsessional, Obsessional please...

Focused, dear, dear Focused
(still in her dressing-gown)
is at the typewriter inside
busy, remote, impatient –
especially with telephone interruptions –

Focused wants to be left alone
to delve into life
to serve up life
raw, stewed-down or evoked

Reassuring of course
will do everything,
cooking, cleaning, urging
everyone to vitamins
and a balance of meals

Complexity goes off to be
Aaaaaah in spite of me
the women in me
                    slip free.

Wherever I Hang

I leave me people, me land, me home
For reasons, I not too sure
I forsake de sun
And de hummingbird splendour
Had big rats in de floorboard
So I pick up me new-world-self
And come, to this place call England
At first I feeling like I in dream –
De misty greyness
I touching de walls to see if they real
They solid to de seam
And de people pouring from de underground system
Like beans
And when I look up to de sky
I see Lord Nelson high – too high to lie

And is so I sending home photos of myself
Among de pigeons and de snow
And is so I warding off de cold
And is so, little by little
I begin to change my calypso ways
Never visiting nobody
Before giving them clear warning
And waiting me turn in queue
Now, after all this time
I get accustom to de English life
But I still miss back-home side
To tell you de truth
I don't know really where I belaang

    Yes, divided to de ocean
    Divided to de bone

Wherever I hang me knickers – that's my home

My Black Triangle

My black triangle
sandwiched between the geography of my thighs

is a bermuda
of tiny atoms
forever seizing
and releasing
the world

My black triangle
is so rich
that it flows over
on to the dry crotch
of the world

My black triangle
is black light
sitting on the threshold of the world
overlooking
all my probabilities

And though
it spares a thought for history
my black triangle
has spread beyond his story
beyond the dry fears of parch-ri-archy

Spreading and growing
trusting and flowing
my black triangle
carries the seal of approval
of my deepest self.

Even Tho

Man I love
but won't let you devour

even tho
I'm all watermelon
and star-apple and plum
when you touch me

even tho
I'm all sea-moss
and jellyfish
and tongue

Come
leh we go to de carnival
You be banana
I be avocado

Come
leh we hug up
and brace-up
and sweet one another up

But then
leh we break free
yes, leh we break free

And keep to de motion
of we own person/ality.

Configurations

He gives her all the configurations
of Europe.

She gives him a cloud burst of parrots

He gives her straight blond hairs
and a white frenzy.

She gives him black wool. The darkness
of her twin fruits.

He gives her uranium, platinum, aluminium
and concorde.

She gives him her 'Bantu buttocks'.

He rants about the spice in her skin.

She croons his alabaster and scratches him.

He does a Columbus –
falling on the shores of her tangled nappy orchard.

She delivers up the whole Indies again
But this time her wide legs close in
        slowly
Making a golden stool of the empire
of his head.

Abra-Cadabra

My mother had more magic
in her thumb
than the length and breadth
of any magician

Weaving incredible stories
around the dark-green senna brew
just to make us slake
the ritual Sunday purgative

Knowing when to place a cochineal poultice
on a fevered forehead
Knowing how to measure a belly's symmetry
kneading the narah pains away

Once my baby sister stuffed
a split-pea up her nostril
my mother got a crochet needle
and gently tried to pry it out

We stood around her
like inquisitive gauldings

Suddenly, in surgeon's tone she ordered,
'Pass the black pepper,'
and patted a little
under the dozing nose

My baby sister sneezed.
The rest was history.

Out of Africa

Out of Africa of the suckling
Out of Africa of the tired woman in earrings
Out of Africa of the black-foot leap
Out of Africa of the baobab, the suck-teeth
Out of Africa of the dry maw of hunger
Out of Africa of the first rains, the first mother.

Into the Caribbean of the staggeringly blue sea-eye
Into the Caribbean of the baleful touristy glare
Into the Caribbean of the hurricane
Into the Caribbean of the flame tree, the palm tree,
the ackee, the high smelling saltfish
and the happy creole so-called mentality.

Into England of the frost and the tea
Into England of the budgie and the strawberry
Into England of the trampled autumn tongues
Into England of the meagre funerals
Into England of the hand of the old woman
And the gent running behind someone
who's forgotten their umbrella, crying out,
'I say...I say-ay.'

from

SUNRIS

(1996)

Introduction to *Sunris*

I am fifteen, leaning through the window of our Princess Street home, having picked up the unmistakable sound of a steel-band coming down – the throbbing boom of the bass, the metallic ringing – and sure enough two minutes later, a lorry full of steel-band men come into being; heads bent intently over pans, oblivious of everything but keeping the pulse of the latest calypso going. Behind them come an ever swelling mass of people, arms linked around necks and waists, a joyous patchwork quilt of bodies dancing or 'tramping' as we called it, under a one o'clock sun shining down in all its inconsiderate glory.

And since I can't bear to be outside such energy, as they move out of sight, I find myself dashing out of the house, down the passageway and onto the streets behind them, pretending not to hear the headmaster-voice of my father shouting from the window: 'Come back here, girl, I say come back.'

Who can keep their daughters forever from the forbidden or more rowdy side of life?

With a slip of my hip, an impulse beyond me, I manage to make an opening for myself within a wave and am quickly embraced – someone's arm around my waist, another's around my shoulders. Thus buoyed and blissed I tramp around the streets of Georgetown in a euphoric rites of passage. That was mini-carnival Guyana-style before independence. Now of course there is the national celebration, 'Mashramani'.

As a child, steelpan, calypso, in fact anything that came from the ordinary folk including the everyday creole speech, were regarded as 'low-class' not only by the colonial powers that be (in our case British) but also by the more snobbish of the upper and middle classes who frowned on folk-culture as common. But despite various measures which included the historical banning of the drum, both carnival and the steel drum continued to flourish. For as David Cuffy noted in his article on carnival:

> ...carnival is a deeply resonant anniversary from the
> bondage of colonial slavery...A journey of freedom as
> well as a mechanism of social release. Its origins escape
> rigid definitions of history and culture. They encom-
> pass European pagan rites, Christian festivals, African
> slavery and the post-emancipation spirit of anger and
> reclamation.

Integral to carnival are the infectious rhythms of the
steel drum and calypso. In the same way that poets such as
Linton Kwesi Johnson, Jean 'Binta' Breeze and Kwame
Dawes have found the rhythms of reggae inspiring, a number
of Caribbean poets have found steel pan and calypso inspir-
ing, the latter both in terms of music and language.

Derek Walcott, St Lucian poet and Nobel Laureate, makes
memorable use of calypso in his 'Spoiler's Return' and in
his plays such as *Joker of Seville*. One also thinks of the
Guyanese poet John Agard's steelpan cycle, *Man to Pan* and
the Trinidadian poet Abdul Malik's *Pan Run*.

Like carnival, calypso feeds on a diversity of strands, from
the use of English nursery rhymes in the earlier Sparrow
calypsos to the more recent incorporation of 'Chutney-Soca',
a coinage of the female Trinidadian East Indian singer,
Drupatee, in which Hindi words and music are mixed with
calypso or the faster soca beat.

I myself have grown up with the words, tunes and
rhythms of calypso constantly in my head – sweet calypso
with its wit, word-play, bravado and gusto. It is the music of
my childhood through which we got the news and scandals
of the day, love and celebration; crime and tragedy, fantasy,
politics, philosophy, in fact all of human experience and all
in the cadences of the people's language, no matter how 'high-
sounding'.

In the *Sunris* poem, I wanted to capture some of the fea-
tures associated with calypso – in terms of tone, directness,
bravado, rhetoric and 'big-word' aspect but breaking out at
times against the two-line rhyming beat. The woman, who
makes the journey of self-naming in the poem, is swept
along by the all-embracing pulse of carnival, rather like the
infectious rhythm of the road-march tune that sets thousands

jumping behind it. While open to the hedonistic pull of carnival, she is always aware of her 'unknown mission' so that her dance becomes a dialectic, her spree a pilgrimage.

In this act of reclaiming the various strands of her heritage she engages with both historical and mythological figures and like the calypsonian sometimes resorts to verbal self-inflation to make her voice heard; 'I think this time I go make history.'

At a personal level the word 'Sunris' resonates with the name of my mother 'Iris' who like her mythic namesake, was for me 'a bridging rainbow'. It also embraces and celebrates my own need for the Sun whose golden 'iris' (though it doesn't come out often) keeps me going in England.

Sunris

Carnival is all that is claimed for it.
It is exultation of the mass will,
its hedonism is so sacred, that to withdraw
from it, not to jump up, to be contemplative
outside of its frenzy is a heresy...
DEREK WALCOTT

Out of the foreday morning –
They coming
Out of the little houses
Clinging to the hillside –
They coming
Out of the big house and the hovel –
They coming
To fill up like mist this pre-Lent morning
To lift up dis city to the sun
To incarnate their own carnation.

Symbol of the emancipated woman I come
I don't care which one frown
From the depths of the unconscious I come
I come out to play – Mas Woman.

This mas I put on is not to hide me
This mas I put on is visionary –
A combination of the sightful sun
A bellyband with all my strands
A plume of scarlet ibis
A branch-of-hope and a snake in mih fist
Join me in dis pilgrimage
This spree that look like sacrilege.

But those who cannot see
Into the intricacies of my blood
better watch they don't put
They foot in they mouth

I'm a hybrid-dreamer
An ancestral-believer
A blood-reveller
Who worship at the house of love.

So Coolieman, Blackman, Redman come,
Potageeman, Chineyman, Whiteman, Brown,
Whoever throw they hand round mih waist
I come out to tasteup mih race
But when I ready I moving free
1 sticking to the flight of my own trajectory
I reaping the flowers of this deep dance mystery
I think this time I go make history.

Hands Hands
Is all a matter of hands
Through the shaping and the cutting
Through the stitching and the touching
Through the bright door of love
Come the splendour of hands.

> *And is dih whole island*
> *Awash in a deep seasound*
> *Is hummingbird possession*
> *Taking flight from dih ground*
> *Is blood beating*
> *And spirit moving free*
> *Is promiscuous wine*
> *Is sanctity.*

Feet Feet
Is all a matter of feet
For the spirits
Take entry from the feet
High-priestess and Devil
Aztec-King and me
Midnight-robber
Saint Theresa,
And Jab-Jab Molassi,
All carried by

      The-rise-and-fall
      The-rise-and-fall

The tranced unstoppable rhythm
And Death mingling free
In his white wing-beats
We ain't stopping
Till Ash Wednesday
Put a kick in we heels.

But O Montezuma,
How could you deliver all the glory
Without a fight?
Gold, you had enough to bribe all heaven,
Paving a haven for our souls.
From the mouth of the Yucatan,
Man. the whole Caribbean.

MONTEZUMA:
Who among us would not have been beguiled?
All the ominous omens and the signs –
A volcano's eruption
The waters of Lake Texaco's rise
A comet sitting like a photograph
No, it was written
In the invisible ink of legend
Across the ageless parchment of the skies.
Feathered-Serpent, Plumed-God,
It was always known that the Great
Quetzalcoatl
Would return to claim his own.

But the radiance, Montezuma,
The shattered radiance
All your temples, codices, Tenochtitlan... gone

MONTEZUMA:

Woman blame the bible and the sword,
Blame the cross of that blood-devouring sun.
Blame the messengers who run
Their relaying marathon –
The fear hammering their chests –
And the picture of that
Half-horse-half-man-God
Which they transmitted to my breast.
Blame the fools bringing me news
Of him who was only Cortez.

I remember it as if I was there,
Montezuma, watching transfixed,
It was as if, legend made flesh
Had descended out of the clouds and mist.
I remember how you tried to woo a return
Sending forth gifts –
A hoop of gold as big as a cartwheel
With engravings of the sun;
A smaller one in silver to signify the moon;
Statues of ocelot, birds, all wrought in gold
You din expect them to turn back...

those conquistadors?

And is dih whole island
Awash in a deep seasound
Is hummingbird possession
Taking flight from dih ground
Is blood beating
And spirit moving free
Is promiscuous wine
Is sanctity.

Streets Streets
Is all a matter of streets
Streets perspire freely
Streets arch back ever so slyly
Streets pulsate
In the deepest centre
Of their asphalt selves
Wave after wave –
Streets shudder and groan;
'Gimmie all the weight and the glory
Fill and trample me
colour and stretch me...
to infinity

O motion in art
Look art in motion
Kanaima and he deathcrew
riding the ocean!

A band of skeletons
With knives in they sides
A mincing apparition
In a menacing sway
Pushing me kinetically
Out of the way
But the road make to walk
On carnival day.

Well if life is a dream
Then I is a dreamer
If is not Papa Bois himself –
The old deer-footed, leaf-bearded curator!
Coming down in a canopy of forest-cool light
Keeper of the green cathedral
(I best be polite)

'Bonjour, Buenos dias,
Good day, Papa Bois,
How the caretaking coming. Sir?'

But the Guardian of the heartland
Barely knowledges the greeting
Brushes an invisible tree-web
Glances upward at his swaying leafy ceiling
Like he intent only on the prayerful breathing
Even in the sea of all this heaving weaving

Roll up de Tassa
Roll up de Tassa, Besessar
Rip up de Tassa, Besessar

O Chutney, offspring of India,
You stirring in your diaspora
Hotter than a Chulha
Hear de Dhantal and de Dholak
Spicing up de Soca

Pour rum
Praise gong
Steel drum
    On fire

Tempo sweet
Rhythm deep
Big-up de beat
    On fire

Iron tone
Move bone
Hips roam
    On fire

Blood hot
Don't stop –
Go to crab-dance
    You must get mud

Father forgive us for we know not,
Forgive the man who just place he hand
on my promiseland
Later he will take the ash and close he eye;
Man born of woman, you born to die.
Spirit preserve my harvest
from their Fat-Tuesday eyes.

Among wings am I
Angels, imps, devil-kings,
Icarus still battling to
Take off in the wind.
Among labyrinth of sounds
Galleries of colour,
It was me of my own free will
Who choose to be embraced by this river.

To enter freely into
                this sweat-of-arms
Wrapped like innocent electrical eels about me

No, nobody tell me it would be easy –
                The rapturous rapids and pitfalls
                                of this journey.

Miracle of Vision!
Who is dis apparition?

If is not Africa herself
Come out to play –
Making dih dance steps
Both of mourning and merriment
On dis carnival day.

Africa, how to begin
After all dis time and water'?
But you know more than me
That spirit must return to spirit
That darkness is
A concentration of light –
So you endure sphinx-like.

Africa, when I remember my father
Pouring a small libation in a corner
Or my mother rounding fufu in in her mortar
The simple burial of a navel-string –
I think of you too and I marvel
How your rituals have survived the crucible –
How they remain with us like relics
In the pillow of our unconscious –
So invigorate me, Africa, with a passing touch
Even as you make your exodus.

History is a river
That flow to the sea
Laced with the bone of memory
I riding high her choreography
I paying homage in ceremony

Yes, I rippling to the music
I slipping pass the ghost ships
Watching old mast turn flowering tree
Even in the heart of all this bacchanal
The Sea returns to haunt this carnival

And is dih whole island
Awash in a deep seasound
Is hummingbird-procession
Taking flight from dih ground
Is blood beating
And spirit moving free
Is promiscuous wine
Is sanctity.

How hammer blows
Can make such tones
How doves can rise
From steel throat
Will always be to me
A sweet oil drum mystery

Underbelly pan
with dih innerbelly
stars
of the underbelly
people
let dih filaments
of your overbelly
sounds
pitch a filter
through blue crest
of old pirate water.

Spread re-echo
regather
down down
wake dih ear
of the middle passage
drown.

Speak to the
Sauteur leap
even as you sweeten
the bones of our
indigenous sleep.

Spread, re-echo
re-gather
round round
touch ground
of Atlantic
brown.

Scatter
like minnows
the shadows
of Jonestown

Underbelly pan
with dih innerbelly
stars
of the underbelly
people
pierce us with
yuh holy steel
make your octaves
to fall on us
like a benediction
of leaves.

Blessed is the first cool shadow of darkness
Blessed is the deep well of our language
Blessed is the space that the spirit inhabit
Blessed is the robe we reserve for it
Blessed is the need of our communion
Blessed is the fire of our consecration.

An is so dih trade winds
urging me with hands of jubilation.
An is so dih trade winds
fanning me with hands of rejuvenation.

An is so I coming in
to dih carnival straights.
Is that Legba playing cripple
by dih crossgates?

Bless my eyesight
Is a whole heap of deity
like they come out to greet me
I think dis time I go make history

Columbus, you is not the only one
who can make discovery
I done unearth
My Mayan mystery

So beat dih iron Ogun
lemme hear dih metal ring
Boom dih bass out Shango
Dih crowd they thundering

Cool me down Yemanja
bathe my face in your river.
Dance yuh dance Kali
destroy, renew me with each blood-shiver
Shiva, Shiva, boy you give me fever

And you too Virgin Mary gyal
shaking up like celebration
I see dih Pope casting doubts
bout your immaculate conception

Iris, Iris, you arcing before me
in a rainbow bridge
Isis, Isis, quintessential one of Egypt
what is that word you waving at me like a script?

O this mas I put on is not to hide me
This mas I put on is visionary,

A combination of the sightful sun
A belly-band with all my strands
A plume of scarlet ibis
A branch of hope and a snake
In my fist.

With the Gods as my judge
And dih people my witness,
Heritage just reach out
And give me one kiss.
From dih depths of dih unconscious
I hear dih snake hiss,
I just done christen myself, SUNRIS.

To the Running of My River
(for Kamal)

Sound the tabla and the sitar!
Pile high my banks
With fruits and flowers –

'Here comes my unsaried daughter
Walking in the simple
Creolisation of herself.

But mark well –
In the black swing of her hair
She is still potential possessee of Kali

In the dusk of her eye
She still keep faith with Diwali
This daughter whose ricegrains

Swell with prosperity even as she moves
In full knowledge of the hard
Ships of her immigrant history.

Listen. To the tremor of India
Still residing
At the bottom of her every speech.

Timehri Airport to Georgetown

Coming down, from Timehri
To Georgetown,
Earth knitted in broader patches
Of a tighter green.

Echoing pull of forest,
Ominous call of jungle.
Road shimmering like waves
Of aluminium in the midday heat.

Smell of earth
Through the half open
Airport taxi window
That and breeze, stiflingly welcome me.

Eyes pinned open
To watermelon, watercoconuts,
Huge papaws dangling like
Bright heavy lanterns from roadside stalls.

Mangoes, drop-pearl stems
I'd almost forgotten,
The splayed dicotyledonous
Of breadfruit leaf.

And coconut tree
Standing like modest intercedary,
Between earth and sky,
Between sky and sea.

The hub of branches –
The long veined leaves,
A supplicant-spider,
Spinning a prayer in its weave.

Blackout

Blackout is endemic to the land.
People have grown sixthsense
and sonic ways, like bats,
emerging out of the shadows
into the light of their own flesh.

But the car headlamps coming towards us
make it seem we're in some thirdworld movie,
throwing up potholes and houses exaggeratedly,
the fresh white painted and grey ramshackle
blending into snug relief.

And inside, the children are still hovering,
hopeful moths around the flickerless Box
immune to the cloying stench of toilets
that can't be flushed. The children,
all waiting on electric-spell to come
and trigger a movie, the one featuring America,
played out endlessly in their heads.

While back outside, coconut vendors decapitate
the night, husky heads cutlassed off
in the medieval glow of bottle lamps.

And everywhere there are flittings
and things coming into being,
in a night where footfall is an act of faith –
A group of young girls huddled in a questionable doorway;
The sudden dim horizontal of an alleyway;

And the occasional generator-lit big house,
obscenely bright –
hurting the soft iris of darkness
in this worn-out movie, slow reeling

Under the endless cinema of the skies.

First Generation Monologue

(an extract)

Like every other Caribbean emigré
who'd put away the lamp of the sun
she spoke of the bad old migrant days:
Yes, it seemed as if the whole of England
was a Scrooge in those days of
four-people-living-in-a-room.
The smell of clothes, dank,
before the only heater.
The white landlady exact as the coin
clanking in the grudging meter.

*

Still I lighted my days
with memories blue as the indigo
of my mother's rinsing water.
I lighted on my memories
like a grasshopper.
Sometimes I was as stranded
as a salmon,
holding my fading hands
before the English fire.
How I longed for the openness of verandahs.

*

The days I got my colours mixed
under that amorphous octopus of a sky –
a dream of colours
on my brain's muddled palette;
Bright blue suddenly brushing grey aside,
slate-roofs glinting galvanise
and everywhere the shimmering
waves of heat,
Evergreens dripping
redblood blossoms at my feet.

*

Europe had become
part of my possession
but how to come to terms
with the architecture?
The walls sealed and solid;
The closed door against the cold;
The ivy of my voice no longer
climbing towards the ceiling –
To overhang green and listening.

*

Where were my days
of leaning through windows
or sitting in the back-steps shade?
Loud ice in lemonade.
Bird-picked mangoes hiding in foliage.
Fowls grazing the backyard
clean-neck, feather-neck,
each solitary.
eyes pulled down –
little photographic hoods
from the glare of the sun.
And Hibiscus, queen of all the flowers,
cupped red and rude against the paling
still glistening with little mercuries
from the earlier shower of earthsmelling rain-
But never enough to keep us rooted.

Long Man

*(For Barbara Cole who first introduced us to the Long Man;
for Jan and Tim who came along, and to*
The Druid Way *by Philip Carr-Gomm)*

On open downland we're as open as he
Me and Jan, Tim and John,
Kalera and Ayesha,
and the cracked-sun
has once again withdrawn
leaving us to windy shawls
and pewtery greys
to newly mowed down
fecund-earth, which the rains
have furrowed into clay.

Plod-Plod
through the caking-blood
of England's sod,
our good shoes growing
sulkier by the minute,
as is my five-year-old,
whose hand, a sixth-sense
tells me to hold,
despite her intermittent tugging
on this our Hill-God pilgrimage.

And even when she manages
to break free, I'm after her
a wiser Demeter –
swift-footed and heavy
with apprehension –
sensing the weald-spirits.
A primitive pull
of the pagan dimension.

'We're off to see the Long Man.
the wonderful Long Man of Wilmington,'
I chant, humouring her
over the timeless witchery
of the landscape.

Meanwhile as always, he's there
looming out of the green coombe
of Windover's womb.

In our heart-searching
and soul-yearning
we stand before him.
But soon our luminous eyes
are nailing him with
a crucifixion of questions
Who and Why and How
he came to be. Male, female,
or ancient presage of androgyny?

With the sun back out
surely he is benevolent Corn-God
and Shepherd of the good harvest?

Sun-in and he's
the Phantom-symbol
of all foreboding;
the Gate-Keeper-Reaper
who would reap us in;
the faceless frozen traveler;
Moon-gazer;
Green-man-mirror
tricking our eyeballs on –
the cunning chameleon.

But going back over
the wet green swelling,
the presumptuous goddess in me

looks back and catches him
off guard –
poor wounded man
the staves in his arms
no barrier for –
She-who-would-break-them
and take him in her arms.

My Northern Sister

(For the Finland-Swedish poet, Edith Södergran, 1892-1923;
who kept faith in her words despite the critics)

Refusing the crown that would wreathe her as dumb,
my Northern-Sister comes, saying, 'It does not
become me to make myself less than I am.'

And she moves into forest
and she brings me out handfuls of snow,
a rugged fir,
a taste of wild thyme,
which is only a taste of her own joyousness –
the fearless gates she keeps open,
including the one for death.

And she gives me heather and pine,
a taste of blue air,
the talking-memory of my own childhood trees,

Weaving a tender chemistry with her red
red heart.

And what have I got to give her?
Only the little thing she says
she's always wanted –
a small letter, to be read on a garden bench
with a cat in the sun.

Edith, my sister, come and sit down

Against the Planet

The ones whose
small hands
once played in our blood

Regard us coldly.
But not so cold to go it alone
on the skien of science,

So up they haul us,
irritated as Jesus
was with his earthly mother;

The way her eyes would fall back
from the greatest works
of his heavenly father

To dwell more wonderingly
upon the infant-hymn
peacefully sleeping

In her lap's shadow.
The ten little stars
of his human toes.

Black

Show me the woman
that would surrender
her little black dress
to a white-robed clan
and I would show you a liar,

Not for their bonfire,
her wardrobe saviour
the number
in which she comes
into her own power.

Go to a funeral
in black and know
that the dead
beside the white candles
will not be offended.

Add amber earrings,
perhaps a hat or scarf of pink
and know you are ready –
for a wedding.
How black absorbs everything.

Stand around at a party
in black – you are your own artist,
your own sensual catalyst,
surprised to say the least
when black brings you

Those sudden inexplicable hostile glances.

White

Never mind how or why –
this slow delight
of waking to a room
that comes out of the
memory of night,
A dusky dawning –
paintings, wardrobe,
hangings…,

Then walking, a sleepwalker,
holding on to walls of vanilla,
great solid slabs
you could sink your mouth into.
The memories of ancestors,
all that blackness
against whiteness.
The starched religiousness of it.

O I could hold
the globe like a face,
Januslike spinning
from the depths of my dreaming
I could face-up
to the stark white page
already seeded
with the best invisible poem.

Wings

*(for John Figueroa, Jamaican poet, inspired by his comment
that as Caribbean people we're preoccupied with Roots,
when maybe we should be signifying ourselves by Wings
– 'Out of the Margins Festival', South Bank, London 1993)*

Consigned to earth
we thought it fitting
to worship only
the sustenance of our roots,
so that when uprootment came
in its many guises
we moved around like
bereaving trees, constantly touching
our sawn-off places.

And though we pretended to be
bright migrant birds
it was always an inward yearning
for the compelling earth
of our roots – lost Africas, Indias,
then the love-tugging land
of our immediate birthmothers.
Past more poignant
than any future.

Root-lovers
Root-grounders
Root-worshippers,
We've been

old hoarding mourners,
constantly counting
our sea-chest of losses,
forgetting the other end
of our green extremis –
the imperishable gift of our wings.

But wasn't it wings
that made our ancestors
climb the airy staircase
whenever they contemplated
rock and a hard place?

And isn't it wings, our own wilful wings,
still taking us into migratory-pull
still taking us into homing-instinct,
beating up the winds
to find our respective havens?

And even if we stay
blissfully or unblissfully still,
in sun-eye or snowflake-kiss
it's still wings taking us back
to the bigger presence of wings.

So wings over you, John,
for your white-bearded
and timely reminder
of our wings.

Icons

Everything foreign was better than local
Or so it seemed when I was a child,
But perhaps the grown-ups lied –
The shimmering lie
Of the emperor's new clothes.

Among the English icons praised to the skies;
Iceapples, Yardleys, Grapes,
The unseen Snowflake.
We'd watch the shopkeeper's crafty hands
Among the apple-crates.

The way he'd carefully
Pull back the crinkled tissue
As if it was cotton-wool
And the glistening red unbittens,
Jewels instead of fruit.

On Christmas morning if we were lucky
We'd delve deep to find an apple-ruby,
Our stocking's only bit of edible magic.
Who knows why I was hardly ever tempted
To bite or ravish.

Even now in England's supermarkets
I instinctively leave the polished red,
A wary Snow White, going instead
For the common locals
Cox's orange-pippins, Russets.

Still, I must say that it gladdens the heart
To see how both my apple-eating daughters
Have emerged, carefully avoiding the pith and pips
While drooling endlessly over the mango
Two sun-starved Eves –

Making a meal of the old creation myth.

Hurricane Hits England

It took a hurricane, to bring her closer
To the landscape
Half the night she lay awake,
The howling ship of the wind,
Its gathering rage,
Like some dark ancestral spectre,
Fearful and reassuring:

Talk to me Huracan
Talk to me Oya
Talk to me Shango
And Hattie
My sweeping, back-home cousin.

Tell me why you visit
An English coast?
What is the meaning
Of old tongues
Reaping havoc
In new places?

The blinding illumination,
Even as you short-
Circuit us
Into further darkness?

What is the meaning of trees
Falling heavy as whales
Their crusted roots
Their cratered graves?

O why is my heart unchained?

Tropical Oya of the Weather,
I am aligning myself to you,
I am following the movement of your winds,
I am riding the mystery of your storm.

Ah, sweet mystery,
Come to break the frozen lake in me,
Shaking the foundations of the very trees
within me,
Come to let me know
That the earth is the earth is the earth.

from

STARTLING THE
FLYING FISH

(2006)

And I Cariwoma
watch my children
take off like
migrating spider-birds
carrying the silver threads
of their linkages,
making of me new
triangulars across Atlantic,
enmeshing me into
their metropolitan affairs –
A thought for one here.
A sigh for one there.
A pride for one somewhere.
Europe? North America?
Smiles at photos
of grands and greatgrands
I've never seen,
the children who shine
like constellations
in my dreams.
For them all I must keep green.
My children are movers.

*

Yet, each decade
something in them
is lost to us.
Something in them
is gained to their places
of adoption.

Life unravels itself
enough to send them home
on a shoestring,

to whine about
streams dried-up
and horizons too narrow
for their eyes' new circumspect.

Astonished to find
children still swimming
like the little porpoises
they once were
in the irretrievable rivers
of their childhood.

Deep
I Cariwoma
have always
carried deep
these islands,
this piece
of Atlantic coastland
inside me.
Sky-deep
Sea-deep
As star is to stone
As tide is to shore
Is just so I hold
these islands
to my coral bones.
And long before
hurricane strike,
some little butterfly,
some little blue messenger
of the soul will ride
the wind to bring
first news to my door.

Yes, I Cariwoma watched history happen
like a two-headed Janus,
however far apart heads can be.

The first head rose up
from the hammock's languorous belly
and turned towards the winged ships
of Columbus's faith,
his bright dreams which soon turned
for us into nightmares.

The other head rose up
from the misery ship, that other hammock,
and swivelled back, locking
as in the deformity of a duenne's foot.
Face as faceless as a duenne,
those bewildered little souls
gazing back in limbo
at the shards of broken pots,
the waves of palmwine betrayal

Only the eyes of the sea-almonds
kept on beckoning –
A cautious welcome across new shores.

But there were other ships
rocked by dreams
and fears and promise

Rolling
with new arrivals
across Atlantic.

From the fields
of Bengal
and Uttar Pradesh,
From Kowloon
and Canton.
From Madeira
and Ireland –

Their indentured mud-
stained feet, soon embroidered
like the slave's instep to the fields.

Their song of exile
their drums of loss
all caught in a weaving odyssey
of no return.
No waiting Penelope
unpicking all her work.

Wind and Shore are my close companions
In my sea-house there are many mansions
Who knows more than me
the songs of the drowning?

Through the artefacts of my shells
I whisper to the living
To the dead I offer a treatise
of continuous remembering –

My memorials between rocks
My altar-places between weeds
Nightly I dance with my children
in the dancehalls of the deep

Islands
Islands
their palm-tree seductions

Pulling tourists like migratory birds –
dwell a moment on these two
women basking on beach-warmth.

One (now in the mid-winter of her life)
claims her husband says
she is no oil painting.

Here with the wide sea, darling,
you can be a dolphin
or newly washed Aphrodite.

And why shouldn't she?
This woman whose red hands
tell their own story.

First-time-Abroad
from England-North,
soak up yourselves
in sunshine and seawater
that will not make you shiver.

No need to know that sea
does not always keep up
this front of blue serenity.

Sitting on the ark of a balcony
facing Atlantic
ocean-spray a heady overture of kisses

Well this is a classic –
the pauses and crashes
the biblical rises

While I like some Mrs Noah stay riveted
trying to still the exuberant waves in me
the movements of pure panic.

Such magnificence will pull something,
and takes it
in the shape of a Canadian tourist

A young male
heading in
despite our crescendo of warning

Surfacing much later on the box
his ecstasy zipped up
his body-bag lifted off

another unreturning dove.

The *Pinta*
The *Niña*
The *Santa María*

The father son and holy ghost
coming across the water –

Three billowing ships
full of adventurers and seasoned sailors
all scrambling around the decks
like mutinous spiders.
All held in check, after three sea-weeks,
by the webbed faith of a stubborn
red-haired Genoese
staring day-in day-out at the horizon.
To turn back now an act of treason.

The *Pinta*
The *Niña*
The *Santa María*
sailing over my tongue's edge in a litany

'*Tierra Tierra*'
that strangled cry
startling the flying fish
and the long sleep of history.

Oceanic voices
rolling through turquoise
to waves of clearness
An invisible life streaming everywhere
just above the grasp of my fingertips –

Is that you Columbus
I discover in a breeze
still startling the flying fish
in search of the Indies?

Genoa, Spain, Lisbon are but a pale memory
to this nautical-shadow floating above blue scales
But how could I have foreseen the dark vistas and the tears
the seeds of destruction that would flourish in discovery's wake?
Or that the name of Amerigo Vespucci would be the necklace
to caress the breast of this continent?
I who near doubled the world and opened
a dazzling seam in Europe's dull vein.
but merely went out convinced
that I had pushed into the Orient.

Ah, it seems as if it were only yesterday
that these islands flowered before me
like a fragrant myth or mirage.
The first I fell upon was Guanahani,
an Indian word which I renamed
San Salvador in honour of our Lord –

Now, even these turquoise waters mock my enterprise
with their Carib name.
Yet if I must be claimed by any
let it be (if they would have me) by the people of the Isles
Here rest my sea-weary bones.
Here haunt my sea-going spirit.

*

Oceanic voices
rolling through turquoise
to waves of clearness –
Voices now harmless as foam

And I Cariwoma
who never speak too ill of the dead
sit listening to the wind unscroll –
old names in old tongues

Guanahani   of the white sands
Liamuiga   of the fertile earth
Wa-omoni   of the heron bird
Kairi   of the humming bird
Kiskeya   of the mountainplace
Alliouagana   of the prickly pear
Madinina   of the flowers
Xaymaca   of wood and water
Iounalao   of the iguana

whose unconquered gaze still bears witness

Still our Cassandra continues
to scream her truth,
each catastrophe coming
through the caul of her vision

Each catastrophe running
the gauntlet of her tongue
only to fall on the walls
of disbelief and disapproval

Helen. A launching of ships.
Greek gifts.
Her sea-resounding voice
picked up by the ears

Of my own middle passage.
My own ships bowing
in prayer across Atlantic.
Her see-far eyes, like mine

Discerning everything –
from those suicidal Carib leaps
down to the soft massacre at Jonestown
all the bloody reincarnations of history.

Her spirit-shrieks. My global shudders.
Her poor mother: 'For godsake girl,
spare me these endless gloomy prophecies
these visions of crumbling towers.'

The people could fly –
See them rise up, a cloud of locusts
or more a host of scarecrows in suneye?
Wind flapping against their
sunworn dresses and tattered shirt-coats

This brethren who lived a life
of saltless endurance.
No slave-food – saltbeef, saltfish,
to blight their blood or mock the freedom,
the heady helium gathering slowly in their veins.

How closely they guarded their levitational-mystery
How calmly they carried out their earthly duties

And now it's lift-off time –
See them making for the
green open hilltops
with nothing but their faith
and their corncobs?

Hear them singing: One bright morning
when my work is over I will fly away home.

The people could fly.
Look! Look, how they coming, Africa!
'Goodbye plantation goodbye'

So that Moon would continue
in its sailing openness

So that Sun would rise up each day
full and replenished

So that Stars would not lose hold
of their gold

So that Moon in fit of jealousy
would not swallow Sun

So that Sun in greedy turn
would not eat-up moon

So that Stars would not put
each other's eyes to the spear

So that Sun, Moon, Stars would not
suddenly vanish

So that the earth would not be plunged
into everlasting darkness – for this

Many an Aztec eye endured
the accumulation of skulls in the plazas

The blood-carpeted steps of the temple.

Gold was their goal
And gold was their God
Gold was their love
And gold was their song
Gold was their thirst
and gold was their hunger
Such golden obsessions
Could only create golden monsters

A king who dusted himself in gold dust each day
before rinsing himself in a gold-silted lake.
A land whose mossy rocks were really
(you guessed it) ingots of pure gold
amber rivers rushing – not towards their own destines
but glistening with the flakes of El Dorado

And whenever they turned towards us
always that conquistadorial yearning
always the same burning question
from their gold-smiting mouths
'The gold in your ears and nose
where did you get it from?
where did you get it from?'

The history books were right
about one thing – we did die like flies.
What they didn't mention was
the mumbled way we cursed ourselves
even as the cord of death tightened
around our breath – we cursed ourselves
more than we cursed them...
for the 'Taino' that came so easy to our lips.

How we still yearn after so many moons
to fight it out in the green arena
skin grating skin like iguanas
without the thunder of those hooves
the cowardice of the canon.

The parrots that mocked us
also mocked them

Their green laughter
Their raucous words

Sucked like shadows
into the invisible kingdom
where all words go.

And you, Malinche,
Now that the fog of these centuries
has started to lift a little – I see you
coming through the weight of history
history with its dates and treaties
history with its goodies and baddies.
Come, my sister, and talk to me.

It is said that you betrayed your people.
That you were the traitor-translator,
the one who with the gift of tongues
bore Cortez an empire as well as a son.
But wasn't it foretold in the ancient prophecies –
that the quetzal would lose its wings
in the fall of Tenochtitlan?

I Malinche, have seen many suns
and many moons of sorrow
my footsteps dogged from childhood
by whispers, rumours, shadows
Perhaps if Popocatepetl or Iztaccihuatl
could speak – not the language of smoke –
but the language of words –

they would tell a different story.
Time and the green jaws of the jungle
have put holes in the leaves of my memory.

Malinchista – they say meaning a sell-out
Malinchista – a word that shadows your name
But how long can we stare into a mirror of blame?
Accept, O prodigal mother of the mestizo –
this marigold flower for the black cloud of your hair.

You there, hummingbird,
my iridescent messenger –
What news now, what revelation,
you pollinating child-of-the-sun.

Boy going to join his mother in Canada
study bad. Turn lawyer.
Girl taking the flower of herself elsewhere.
Turn nurse. Maybe doctor.
Whole families sucked abroad.

Through the glass of the departure lounge
old canecutter watches it all
face a study of diasporic brooding.
Watches the silver shark
waiting on the tarmac.

Watches until the shuddering monster
takes off with his one
and only grandson –
leaving behind a gaping hole
in the glittering sea we call sky.

But now outside the airport building
where emotions are no longer checked in,
the old man surrenders
to his gut-instinct,
sinking to his knees on the grass.

His cane-shot eyes
his voice cracked as he wails
what his bones know for certain:
'*Nevaar* to meet again
Nevaar to meet again'

Come, Hanuman,
only your many arms
can help console this man –
still waving to an empty sky
the white flag of his handkerchief.

Yes, through it all
Cane still dancing
green in sun and breeze
still glistening and rippling –
No matter how we
burn and chop him
no matter how we
crush and boil him
no matter how we
curse and blame him
Next year he up again
hands in the air
waving fresh-fresh as ever
a carefree carnival character –.
Mr Midas, the man
with the golden touch
or better yet
original alchemist
spilling his crystal-seed
his tiny jewels
of transformation
at our weeping feet.

Resting my face against
the soft flames of your petals
breathing in your subtle
almost no-smelling fragrance
touching your stigma, stamen, pollen,
touching your dark green
serrated leaves that gently support
your inexpressible beauty
your unquenchable thirst for sun and rain.

Hibiscus – everywhere
red, open and not without sorrow
like your people.

Sly Anansi know how to tease me,
like that time he sense

My second-thoughts shift
about the propriety of our tryst.

Hear he, fingers
moonlighting on my knee;

'Woman shouldn't think you know,
Woman should just act.

Too much thinking-thinking
can lead to dry river valley,

Woman is nature and nature is power.
Eh! Eh! When nature shrug we run fuh cover.

No, thinking does not lead
to peak-experience ecstasy.'

Hmmm...
I thinking all the same

How I can use weave of words
to bend web of laws,

How I can submit papers,
inserting clause –

In other words, how I can make
full claim on cyclone, storm, hurricane –

And every eddy eddying forth
from my warm unstable edges.

Yes, how I can keep clear conscience
while easing the low pressures

Rising natural-natural
from my interfrontal zone.

And why shouldn't I let myself
be possessed by the gods?
Why shouldn't I open myself
to their amorous advances?
They who never think
that a woman is past it.
They for whom whiling away
some time with a mortal
is but a drop in eternity's ocean.

Zeus, Zeus
whatever happen between us
is we business.

From the fortress of its buttress
right up to its wide
spreading branches
Silk Cotton Tree
breathes standoffishness –

Not the kind of tree, my friend,
to threaten with an axe.
They say canoe hacked from its trunk
bound to meet a sticky end.
Not the kind of tree to gather round
for test match post-mortem
or hang about aimless and boldface
like those young men
mouthing their soft obscenities
under its wounded shade –
testing, I tell you, the patience of legend.

The sleep-inducing rain
beating down on the galvanise
is just iron-man Ogun
turning his hand to steelpan

The clatter of wind in the trees
is just Oya scattering her vocals
among an acoustics of leaves

The rolling and receding thunder
is just Shango hitting his old drum-kit
with some new lightning-riffs.

The way the red sun surrenders

its wholeness to curving ocean

bit by bit. The way curving ocean

gives birth to the birth of stars

in the growing darkness,

wearing everything in its path

to cosmic smoothness.

The impulse of stones rolling

towards their own roundness.

The unexpected comets of flying fish.

And Forest, Great-Breathing-Spirit,

rooting to the very end

for the life of this planet.

Follow that painting back –
the long forgotten one
still gracing this Big House wall.
The gilded frame, the tones and shades,
old gold and browns –
just who is this autumnal English gentleman?
This baccra-ancestor –
his pastoral-pose now abandoned to plantation ghosts.

By all means note with care
the dead hare lying at his feet,
the cobwebbed-symmetry of his hunting gun
and good dog looking up, knowing its place
in empire's scheme of things.

And further back behind those Elizabethan curtains –
our own unframed drama of flames and whips –
an old-world new-world saga of lost and pillage.
And though I Cariwoma prefer not to dwell
on the wrongs of history, I must bear witness –
to the invisible frieze of lips.
To sculptural hurts which I must try to heal
if only with my balm of words.

How good to see the sunshine
still in your eyes –
my come-home-to-visit daughter.
How good to know that the cold
hasn't put on you – a dampener.

Your arms still bringing gift-hugs.
Your face hanging like a lamp
onto my every story-telling word.

Surely for you, Moon-Gazer will turn up
once more outside your window?
Surely for you, Mama-Wata
will make her subtle
splash more audible?
And everywhere flowers will re-bloom
their names on your memory.

Many have stamped themselves
with the ink of exile.
But you, my daughter
from a land of many waters –
belong to the world.

The children of Las Margaritas
in the State of Chiapas are dancing
but who are they honouring,
hands raised towards the heavens?
Is it the rain-god, Tlaloc?
Is it Mary or Jesus?
Is it the goddess of the ripening
maize, Chicomecoatl?

Like their ancestors before them,
who have themselves become deities
through their suffering and dying –
the children of Las Margaritas
in the State of Chiapas are dancing;
have entered the dance.

They are dancing for freedom, for bright
Quetzal colours.
They are dancing for justice, recompense
for old and new violations.
They are dancing for themselves,
here, on this plateau, with the rains
drifting down from the mountains.

Sea right here on your lipshore
is where I Cariwoma must come
to reacquaint with all of me.
Right here on your shifting sands
is where I must face up
to life's cosmic exclamations.
So come Sea, make we catch up
on all the labrish since you last see me –
Let me hear once more your mouthwash
echoes in my own voicespeak.

Today I sing of Sea self
a glittering breathing
in a turquoise dress

Constantly stitched and re-stitched
by the bright seamstresses of flying fish
adding a thousand sapphire touches

With no boat or ship to darken
the hem of her horizon
no shadows cast

Just the straight rising sun
Sea memory is as clear
as a desert island

And I am on the edge
of this new world
awaiting the footprints of my arrival

POEMS FOR
YOUNGER READERS

Sun Is Laughing

This morning she got up
on the happy side of bed,
pulled back the grey sky-curtains
and poked her head
through the blue window
of heaven,
her yellow laughter
spilling over,
falling broad across the grass,
brightening the washing on the line,
giving more shine
to the back of a ladybug
and buttering up all the world.

Then, without any warning,
as if she was suddenly bored,
or just got sulky
because she could hear no one
giving praise
to her shining ways,
Sun slammed the sky-window close
plunging the whole world
into greyness once more.

O Sun, moody one,
how can we live
without the holiday of your face?

Headmistress Moon

I'm headmistress
of this school they call the night.
I float among my star-pupils
who are all very bright.
When I ring my moon-bell,
everyone pays attention,
the lesson begins with a silent spell,
and then a sparkling concentration.

But sometimes I seriously think
of giving up the headship –
retiring to a cosmic retreat
and putting up my blooming feet.

In the Great Womb-Moon

In the great womb-moon
I once did swoon

Time was a millennium
In my mother's belly

There was water
There was tree
There was land
There was me

Time was a millennium
In my mother's belly

There was planet
There was star
There was light
There was dark

Time was a millennium
In my mother's belly
How I frogkicked
And I frolicked
Like a cosmic
Little comic...

Then came a century, the water subsided,
I was forced out like a morning-star
Into the borders of another world.
I'm not unhappy, but sometimes,
There's a wee mourn in me for the time when –

Time was a millennium
In my mother's belly

Baby-K Rap Rhyme

My name is Baby-K
An dis is my rhyme
Sit back folks
While I rap my mind;

Ah rocking with my homegirl,
My Mommy
Ah rocking with my homeboy,
My Daddy
My big sister, Les, an
My Granny,
Hey dere people – my posse
I'm the business
The ruler of the nursery

poop po-doop
poop-poop po-doop
poop po-doop
poop-poop po-doop

Well, ah soaking up de rhythm
Ah drinking up my tea
Ah bouncing an ah rocking
On my Mommy knee
So happy man so happy

poop po-doop
poop-poop po-doop
poop po-doop
poop-poop po-doop

Wish my rhyme wasn't hard
Wish my rhyme wasn't rough
But sometimes, people
You got to be tough

Cause dey pumping up de chickens
Dey stumping down de trees
Dey messing up de ozones
Dey messing up de seas
Baby-K say, stop dis –
please, please, please

poop po-doop
poop-poop po-doop
poop po-doop
poop-poop po-doop

Now am splashing in de bath
With my rubber duck
Who don't like dis rhyme
Kiss my baby-foot
Babies everywhere
Join a Babyhood

Cause dey hotting up de globe, man
Dey hitting down de seals
Dey killing off de ellies
For dere ivories
Baby-K say, stop dis –
please, please, please

poop po-doop
poop-poop po-doop
poop po-doop
poop-poop po-doop

Dis is my Baby-K rap
But it's a kinda plea
What kinda world
Dey going to leave fuh me?
What kinda world
Dey going to leave fuh me?

Poop po-doop

Give Yourself a Hug

Give yourself a hug
when you feel unloved

Give yourself a hug
when people put on airs
to make you feel a bug

Give yourself a hug
when everyone seems to give you
a cold-shoulder shrug

Give yourself a hug –
a big big hug

And keep on singing,
'Only one in a million like me
Only one in a million-billion-trillion-zillion
like me.'

Cat-Shots

Sitting upright
with her legs
well together –
a beautiful vase
that doesn't need
a flower.

*

Lying on the fish-tank
like the Guardian of Fish,
looking so benevolent
but there's a deep fish-wish.

*

Behind the curtains
on the window-sill,
an actress pacing
just before the show begins.

*

Standing by the door
like a real little muggins,
wanting to stay out
yet wanting to come in.

Cat-Rap

Lying on the sofa
all curled and meek
but in my furry-fuzzy head
there's a rapping beat.
Gonna rap while I'm napping
and looking sweet
gonna rap while I'm padding
on the balls of my feet

Gonna rap on my head
gonna rap on my tail
gonna rap on my
you know where.
So wave your paws in the air
like you just don't care
with nine lives to spare
gimme five right here.

Well, they say that we cats
are killed by curiosity,
but does this moggie mind?
No, I've got suavity.
When I get to heaven
gonna rap with Macavity,
gonna find his hidden paw
and clear up that mystery.

Nap it up
scratch it up
the knack is free
fur it up
purr it up
yes that's me.

The meanest cat-rapper you'll ever see.
Number one of the street-sound galaxy.

Sleeping Out

What it is we cats get up to
when we don't come home?

What do we do? Where do we go?
Bet you humans would like to know.

Do we make a magic circle
recite poetry, dance and chortle?

Do we form an ancient pack
and prey along the railway track?

Do we set the night on fire
eyes emerald, sapphire?

Do we have a brawling, fur-flying,
caterwauling old knees-up?

Do we find a partner
and have a lovey-dovey smooch-up?

Or do I, bit-of-a-loner,
slink off under the warmth
of a parked car for shelter?

That's for me to know and you to wonder.

Me and Mister Polite

Again and again
we met in the lane

We met in the sunshine
We met in the rain
We met in the windy
We met in the hail
We met in the misty
And autumn-leaf trail
On harsh days and dark days
On days mild and clear

And if it was raining
He'd say, 'Nice weather for ducks'
And if it was sunny
He'd say, 'Good enough for beach-wear'
And if it was windy
He'd say, 'Could do without that wind'
And if it was nippy
He'd say, 'Nippy today'
And if it was cold-windy-rainy-grey
(which it nearly always was)
He'd say, 'Horrible day'
Or 'Not as good as it was yesterday'

And he'd hurry away with a brief tip of his hat
His rude dog pulling him this way and that.

Turner to His Critic

(who dismissed his painting, 'Snow Storm – Steam Boat Off
a Harbour's Mouth' 1842 as 'soapsuds and whitewash'. Turner was
said to have tied himself to the mast of a ship to experience a snowstorm)

Soapsuds and whitewash, Critic?
Man, don't make me livid!
I was tied in a snowstom
To the mast of a ship.
Do you have the foggiest of it?
Do you know what it is to be buffeted?
The buzzard of a blizzard
And the waves churning over me.
The wildness of the whirlwind
The horses foaming at my feet.
Why even Sea can see
Through her storm-spectacles
That this work is a masterpiece.
Soapsuds and whitewash indeed!

If I had my way, you, Sir would be
Soap-sudded to the bottom of the sea.

Come On into My Tropical Garden

Come on into my tropical Garden
Come on in and have a laugh in
Taste my sugar cake and my pine drink
Come on in please come on in

And yes you can stand up in my hammock
and breeze out in my trees
you can pick my hibiscus
and kiss my chimpanzees

O you can roll up in the grass
and if you pick up a flea
I'll take you down for a quick dip-wash
in the sea
believe me there's nothing better
for getting rid of a flea
than having a quick dip-wash in the sea

Come on into my tropical garden
Come on in please come on in

Mama-Wata

Down by the seaside
when the moon is in bloom
sits Mama-Wata
gazing up at the moon

She sits as she combs
her hair like a loom
she sits as she croons
a sweet kind of tune

But don't go near Mama-Wata
when the moon is in bloom
for sure she will take you
down to your doom.

For Forest

Forest could keep secrets
Forest could keep secrets

Forest tune in every day
to watersound and birdsong
Forest letting her hair down
to the teeming creeping of her forest-ground

But Forest don't broadcast her business
no Forest cover her business down
from sky and fast-eye sun
and when night come
and darkness wrap her like a gown
Forest is a bad dream woman

Forest dreaming about mountain
and when earth was young
Forest dreaming of the caress of gold
Forest rootsing with mysterious Eldorado

and when howler monkey
wake her up with howl
Forest just stretch and stir
to a new day day of sound

but coming back to secrets
Forest could keep secrets
Forest could keep secrets

And we must keep Forest

Wha Me Mudder Do

Mek me tell you wha me mudder do
wha me mudder do
wha me mudder do

Me mudder pound plaintain mek fufu
Me mudder catch crab mek calaloo stew

Mek me tell you wha me mudder do
wha me mudder do
wha me mudder do

Me mudder beat hammer
Me mudder turn screw
she paint chair red
then she paint it blue

Mek me tell you wha me mudder do
wha me mudder do
wha me mudder do

Me mudder chase bad-cow
with one 'Shoo'
she paddle down river
in she own canoe
Ain't have nothing
dat me mudder can't do
Ain't have nothing
dat me mudder can't do

Mek me tell you

Granny Granny Please Comb My Hair

Granny Granny please comb my hair
you always take your time
you always take such care

You put me on a cushion between your knees
you rub a little coconut oil
parting gentle as a breeze

Mummy Mummy
she's always in a hurry-hurry
rush
she pulls my hair
sometimes she tugs

But Granny
you have all the time
in the world
and when you're finished
you always turn my head and say,
'Now who's a nice girl?'

Don't Cry Caterpillar

Don't cry, Caterpillar
Caterpillar, don't cry
You'll be a butterfly – by and by.

Caterpillar, please
Don't worry 'bout a thing

'But,' said Caterpillar,
'Will I still know myself – in wings?'

Ar-a-rat

I know a rat on Ararat
He isn't thin, he isn't fat
Never been chased by any cat
Not that rat on Ararat.
He's sitting high on a mountain breeze
Never tasted any cheese
Never chewed up any old hat
Not that rat on Ararat.
He just sits alone on a mountain breeze
Wonders why the trees are green
Ponders why the ground is flat
O that rat on Ararat.
His eyes like saucers, glow in the dark –
The last to slip from Noah's ark.

Teenage Earthbirds

Flying by
on the winged-wheels
of their heels

Two teenage earthbirds
skateboarding
down the street

Rising
unfeathered –
in sudden air-leap

Defying law
death and gravity
as they do an ollie

Landing back
in the smooth swoop
of youth

And faces gaping,
gawking, impressed
and unimpressed

Only mother watches – heartbeat in her mouth.

Book-heart

The books I love
are well fingered and thumbed
have tiny butter smudges
may harbour a crumb
the odd cat-whisker
a few dog-ears
a drop of tear
a brownish stain
(that looks suspiciously like tea)

I for one, am glad to say,
do not judge a book
by its cover –
but flit first among its leaves
like a hummingbird
sipping at a flower

The books I love
I must admit
do not sit
behind a museum of glass.
No the books I love
get kissed and squeezed
and pressed against my heart.

GLOSSARY

'i is a long-memoried woman' owes its inspiration to a dream I had one night of a young African girl swimming to the Caribbean with a garland of flowers around her. When I woke up I interpreted this to mean that she was trying to cleanse the ocean of the pain and suffering that she knew her ancestors had gone through in that traumatic transatlantic crossing of slaves from Africa to the New World:

> Even in dreams I will submerge myself
> swimming like one possessed
> back and forth across that course
> strewing it with sweet smelling flowers –
> one for everyone who made the journey

Kra: In African cosmology, Kra is taken to mean 'soul', the divine essence that cannot die.

Skin-Teeth: A grin that masks true feelings.

Massa: A creolised name for 'Master' usually used in a mocking way. Such as the political slogan, 'Massa Day Done'.

Skinless Higue: From the word 'hag', a scary supernatural old woman who supposedly changes herself into a ball of fire and sucks the blood of young children, a vampire-like figure.

Anancy: Trickster/shapeshifter spider-man of West African and Caribbean folklore.

Amalivaca: Amerindian god, to whom rock paintings (Timehri) are attributed.

Kai: An Amerindian chief who sacrificed himself to a waterfall to save his tribe. His name lives on in Kaieteur, the Guyana waterfall with the world's longest perpendicular drop.

Makonaima: A culture hero among the Carib tribes of Guyana.

Chigger: A burrowing bloodsucking flea that lays its eggs under human skin, especially between the toes.

THE FAT BLACK WOMAN'S POEMS

Candlefly: Another name for a firefly. Tiny insect with a blinking light.

Golden-stool: Stool made of solid gold, sacred symbol of Ashanti nationhood.

Nation-language: An expression for creole broadly speaking coined by Barbadian poet, Kamau Braithwaite, highlighting the fact that the slaves belonged to various 'nations' such as Akan or Ashanti.

LAZY THOUGHTS OF A LAZY WOMAN

'Wherever I Hang', '*Yes, divided to the ocean / divided to the bone*': An echo of Derek Walcott's 'divided to the vein' in his poem 'A Far Cry from Africa'

'My Black Triangle': A playful appropriation of the description for the triangular slave route – Europe-Africa-Caribbean.

Narah: East Indian in origin. An abdominal pain for which massaging with oil is the traditional remedy to realign the muscles.

Gauldings: A long-legged egret seen along the Guyana coastland, especially feeding off the ticks of cows.

SUNRIS

Jab Jab: From the French diable (devil). A Carnival character smeared in molasses.

Midnight Robber: An outrageous character with an elaborate cape and famous for his inflated speeches of empty threats, hence *Robber Talk*.

Montezuma: Aztec emperor in power at the time of the arrival of the Spanish conquistadors in the early 16th Century. Cortés, leader of the Spanish invaders, was looked upon as the returning God, Quetzalcoatl, through a series of bizarre coincidences.

Kanaima: Amerindian supernatural figure of death and spirit of vengeance.

Papa Bois: Caribbean folk figure. A Pan-like cloven-footed custodian of the forest who objects to its wanton destruction.

Chulha: Hindi word for stove.

Roll Up De Tassa: The Tassa is a drum used at East Indian ceremonies. 'Roll up de tassa, Besessar' became a chorus line popularised by the Soca singer Drupattie, famous for her 'Chutney Soca'.

Sauteur Leap: From the French *sauter* (to leap). A historic landmark in the once French-ruled island of St Lucia and from where Caribs resisted enslavement by leaping to the sea that bears their name.

Jonestown: Named after the American pastor Jim Jones, a cult figure who set up a community of followers in the interior of Guyana that ended in the mass suicide of hundreds in 1980.

Legba, Ogun, Oya: All belong to the Yoruba pantheon of gods and *Shango, Yemanja* goddesses. *Legba*, associated with the crossroads and communication; *Ogun* with war and metal work; *Oya* with the wind and sweeping change; *Yemanja* with oceans, rivers and motherhood; *Shango* with thunder and his double-sided axe.

Kali: Hindu 'Dark Mother' goddess with her necklace of skulls, identified with destruction and dynamic energy.

Shiva: Hindu Lord of the Dance.

Iris: Greek goddess of the rainbow.

Isis: Egyptian goddess, usually depicted with solar disc and horns of a cow. Known as the Mistress of Magic.

Long-Man: A giant figure carved into the chalky hillside of the Sussex Downs. The Long Man of Wilmington, as he is known, is said to be the work of the monks of Wilmington Priory in the Middle Ages, though others say he may be Celtic or Saxon in origin.

Moon-Gazer: A tall supernatural figure of Guyana folklore. He stands astride the crossroads, gazing at the full moon, and all are advised not to attempt to pass through the arch of his legs.

STARTLING THE FLYING FISH

Duenne: Spirit of unbaptised child that wanders the forest goblin-like with feet turned backwards.

Macchu Picchu: Fortified city, high above the Urubamba River. A ruined complex of terraces, gabled houses and sacred plazas carved out in the Andes that bear witness to Inca architecture.

Intihuatana: Stone pillar, a type of sundial found at Macchu Picchu. The word itself means 'Hitching post for the sun'. It was the place to which the priests tied the sun at at the point of its furthest distance from the southern hemisphere (winter solstice) so that it would begin to come back again.

Chachalaka: Bird hunted and domesticated by the Indians.

Cassava: The root-vegetable, manioc.

Wapishana/Macusi/Warrau: Names of some of the Amerindian tribes in Guyana.

Pork-knocker: Prospector for gold or diamonds in the rivers of the Guyana hinterland. Salted pork, a regular part of their diet, hence the nickname.

El Dorado: Fabled city of gold that lured European explorers to the rivers and mountains of South America during the 16th and early 17th centuries. Rumours of this wealthy kingdom based on the Golden Man (El Hombre Dorado) – a magnificent king who would wash gold dust from his skin in the middle of a lake.

Atahualpa: The Inca ruler at the time of Pizarro's invasion of Peru. Regarded with fear and awe by his people as a direct descendant of the sun.

Montezuma: Aztec Emperor who bestowed gifts on the conquistadores in the hope that the strangers would leave. He believed the Spaniard Cortés to be a reincarnation of the exiled Quetzalcoatl, a culture hero and Lord of the Dawn.

Quetzal: Feathers of the Quetzal bird, like jade, were precious to the Aztecs.

Xocolatl: Special drink made from the beans of the cacao which was both a food and a form of currency.

Cacahuaquchtl: Mayan name for the cacao tree.

Quetzalcoatl: The Toltec god/king, the Plumed Serpent who brought the gift of learning and the seeds of the divine chocolate-giving cacao.

Papa Bois: A Pan-like cloven-foot father-protector of the forest and its creature inhabitants.

Guanahani (San Salvador), *Liamuiga* (St Kitts), *Wa-omoni* (Barbuda), *Kairi* (Trinidad), *Kiskeya* (Dominican Republic), *Alliouagana* (Montserrat), *Madinina* (Martinique), *Xaymaca* (Jamaica), *Iounalao* (St Lucia): original Amerindian names of these Caribbean islands.

Tiano: Arawak word meaning peace.

Aciguatao: Taino word meaning to be sad.

Kokolia: Taino name for a sea crab.

Warawao: Red-tailed hawk (Taino).

Tenochtitlan: Original Mexican capital whose splendour greatly impressed the Spanish conquistadors.

Popcatepetl and Iztaccihuatl: twin volcanoes looming above Mexican city. Their names meaning 'Smoking Mountain' and 'White Lady'.

Malinche: Amerindian woman who was the translator for Hernan Cortés during the Spanish Conquest of 1521. She was 'given to him as a gift' and bore him a son who is seen symbolically as the first *mestizo*, a child of Amerindian and Spanish blood. *Malinchista* later became an insulting expression for betrayal.

Anancy: Mythical shape-shifting spider of West African cosmology and the wily trickster figure of West Indian Anancy folktales.

Hanuman: Loyal monkey of Hindu mythology.

Silk-Cotton Tree: Also known as the Ceiba and Kapok tree. An enormous tree that grows both in Africa and the Caribbean. Said to attract ancestral spirits and linked to a number of superstitions.

Baccra: Creole term for a white person.

Tlaloc: Atzec Rain God.

Chicomecoatl: Mexican corn Goddess.

Persephone: Daughter of Zeus and Demeter (agricultural goddess) who was snatched by Hades to the underworld. Through the pleas of her mother to the other gods she was allowed back each year (Spring and Summer).

Penelope: Wife of Odysseus who remained true to him during his long absence. She was besieged with suitors who had moved into the palace. Penelope had promised to choose one of them as king when she was finished weaving a tapestry. But what she wove by day she unravelled by night.

Cassandra: Prophetess who spoke the truth but fated never to be believed.